Original title:
Breezes and Palms

Copyright © 2025 Creative Arts Management OÜ
All rights reserved.

Author: Riley Donovan
ISBN HARDBACK: 978-1-80581-674-4
ISBN PAPERBACK: 978-1-80581-201-2
ISBN EBOOK: 978-1-80581-674-4

Lush Fronds in Twilight

Under fading light, they dance so free,
Wobbling like jelly, quite funny to see.
Laughter echoes where shadows play,
As leaves conspire to steal the day.

A palm joked with a tire swing, you see,
'Why swing with whoosh, when you can swing with me?'
Their whispering leaves share giggles galore,
As the twilight giggles, wanting more.

Waves of Tranquility

The surf laughs softly, a ticklish tease,
Hit your toes, then back with ease.
Like friends who chase and pull away,
They beckon at first light of day.

A seagull swoops with a belly flop,
Squawking wildly, a flappy crop.
Shells scatter like they're on a spree,
Running away, but where's the glee?

Shadows of Swaying Green

In the heat of noon, they wiggle and sway,
Casting odd shapes that lead minds astray.
A silhouette here, a dance more bold,
Feeling quite silly, they laugh uncontrolled.

One leaf called out to a bug on the ground,
'You stop right there, don't scoot around!'
They giggled and twirled in the sunlight's rays,
Shadows performing their quirky displays.

A Breath of Salt and Sand

Footprints giggle as waves come to play,
Puppies bark back at the seagulls in sway.
A crab in a hurry, what's it trying to do?
With tiny pinchers, it shouts, 'Not you!'

The sunbeam waves with a wink and a grin,
'Catch me if you can, that is where to begin.'
Sandcastles tumble, 'Who needs a moat?'
The tide runs for cover, 'Oh dear!' it wrote.

Shimmering Stories of the Earth

The swaying trees swing jokes anew,
They giggle and whisper, who knew?
Leaves rustle loud, a comedic play,
Nature's humor on full display.

Squirrels wear shades, acting so cool,
While birds form a band, breaking the rule.
The breeze blows by with a cheeky grin,
Inviting all to jump right in.

Twilight's Fresh Exhale

As daylight fades, the shadows dance,
Critters prance about in a silly trance.
Fireflies flicker as if on strike,
Demanding attention, they're quite the tyke.

The moon rolls in with a sparkling laugh,
"Let's play tag!" says a raccoon on the path.
Stars wink above, a whimsical scene,
Nature's comedy, a joyous routine.

Nature's Breath on Skin

Skin tickled by whispers, soft and sly,
A spider swings by, oh my, oh my!
Pollen decides to play hide and seek,
While daisies toss jokes, cheeky and freak.

The sun peeks down, not one to pout,
Says, "I'll tan your nose, just watch out!"
And in this light-hearted, sunny affair,
Laughter flows freely, lost in the air.

Solstice under Starry Canopy

Gather round, it's a jolly scene,
With critters and humans, we're a wild machine.
The stars chuckle down, shiny and bright,
As everyone bonds in the soft moonlight.

A campfire cracks jokes, s'mores in the mix,
While crickets hold auditions for their new flicks.
Nature's a stage, and we're all here
To laugh and enjoy as the night draws near.

Soothing Symphony of The Expanse

In the meadow, ducks quack loud,
As I chase them through the crowd.
A breeze whispers to my hat,
Off it flies! Oh, imagine that!

Friends and I dance like fools,
Balancing drinks as we use tools.
The air carries laughter here and there,
As lemonade stains faces with flair.

Sunshine rolls, a playful tease,
My shorts wave, caught in the breeze.
We spin like tops, then collide,
In this wacky, wild joyride!

The sunset's glow, a clownish sight,
Our shadows stretch in the fading light.
With each chuckle, the day takes flight,
And the night awaits with giggles so bright.

Gossamer Veils of Silken Air

A lazy cat on a sunny ledge,
Prowls like a lion near the hedge.
With a flip, she lands in my lap,
Oh, this is a cozy nap trap!

Wind chimes sing a silly tune,
Dancing rhymes with the afternoon.
My drink spills, and it's all a mess,
But oh, how we laugh at our stress!

Chasing kites like little kids,
Tangled strings and silly bids.
A flock of birds flies overhead,
"Why fly in formation?"—I said!

The stars appear, our laughing eyes,
Make wishes on the moonlit skies.
With every twinkle, more giggles soar,
Underneath the night, we'll sing for more!

Hush of the Evening Breeze

In twilight's glow, the antics start,
A squirrel on a branch, oh what art!
With acorn hats, they twirl and dance,
Even the shadows join the prance.

A breeze whispers secrets, quite absurd,
Telling tales that are hardly heard.
Leaves giggle softly, tease the night,
As crickets chirp with sheer delight.

Flights of Fancy Beneath the Sun

A kite soars high, with colors bright,
It dives and loops, a silly sight.
The kids all laugh, they pull and tug,
While one gets stuck—a very big bug!

Sunlight gleams on slippery grass,
With running shoes, they go flying past.
One takes a tumble, arms flail like wings,
And giggles erupt, oh the joy it brings!

The Art of Gentle Motion

A hammock sways like a sleepy cat,
While someone's stuck, imagine that!
The more they wiggle, the more they cling,
It's a battle of wills in this lazy swing.

Chairs squeak funny, they rock and sway,
As laughter fills up the sunny day.
With every creak, a joke is shared,
In this slapstick show, no one is spared!

Tides of Tranquility

At the shore, the seagulls scheme,
As someone drops their ice cream.
With flapping wings and squawking loud,
It's a feathery frenzy, they gather a crowd.

Waves crash softly, they dance with glee,
But one gets splashed—what a sight to see!
With laughter that echoes all around,
In this wave of joy, pure fun is found.

The Poetry of Frond and Fleece

A frond jumps up, it takes a bow,
With every gust, it shows us how.
The sun rolls in, a shining spy,
While clouds just giggle, drifting by.

A squirrel poses, oh so spry,
He thinks he's suave, but oh my, my.
A leaf lets loose, it starts to sway,
And catches him, in quite the play!

The shadows dance on sandy ground,
As laughter blends with nature's sound.
A coconut falls with a comic thud,
And rolls away just like a dud!

In this wild scene where chaos reigns,
Nature's laughter fills the plains.
So tip your hat to joyous sights,
Where every twist brings pure delights.

Skyward Glances Among Tropical Leaves

Up in the air, the chatter flies,
As critters plot beneath clear skies.
They scheme and dream of snacks galore,
While sunlight tickles every shore.

A seagull swoops, with style, no doubt,
His dive is sharp, his wig is stout.
But just below, a fishy prank,
Glimmers in water, a playful prank!

The breeze can't help but crack a grin,
As flowers giggle, oh what a win!
With colors bright and scents so sweet,
They sway together in rhythmic beat.

Amidst the fun, the shadows tease,
For nature's laughter rides the breeze.
So lift your gaze, and join the game,
Where joy and cheer know no shame.

Layers of Light and Freedom

A flicker here, a shadow there,
The sun plays peek, without a care.
While little critters play charades,
Under the light, in leafy shades.

The lizards dance, yes, they are sly,
They leap and twirl, oh my! Oh my!
A sudden flop, a tumble too,
Yet on they go, with quite the view!

A breeze must gossip, that's its fate,
It whispers tales of love and hate.
As petals flirt, and seeds take flight,
With giggles shared, in morning light.

So join the fun, let spirits soar,
In nature's play, there's always more.
With every step, a tale unfolds,
In laughter's arms, be brave and bold.

Coastal Tales of the Gentle Whirl

Once upon a wave, the crabs conspired,
To steal the show, they felt inspired.
With tiny claws and sideways dance,
They practiced hard, not left to chance.

The gulls above, they just can't stare,
As crabs do twirls, without a care.
But nature's floors have surprises too,
A wayward wave, a shocked "Boo hoo!"

Sunsets blush, the sky ignites,
While critters gather for evening bites.
With laughter echoing through the air,
A symphony of joy everywhere.

So join the crabs with wiggles grand,
Embrace the shore, take nature's hand.
In flip-flops, sandals, or in bare feet,
We dance together, life's oh so sweet!

Gentle Caress of the Sea

A tickle from waves, they splash with glee,
They dance and they sway, as spry as can be.
Seagulls squawk loudly, they hurl back their jokes,
While fishermen grumble, lost all of their hooks.

The sandcastles crumble, a tragic mistake,
As kiddos get soaked, oh, what a ruckus to make!
Flip-flops go flying, a tragic retreat,
As laughter erupts from their sandy defeat.

The beach ball goes soaring, a high-flying feat,
While sunburned folks grumble, "This sun's just too sweet!"
But there's joy in the screams of a kite in the air,
As tides snicker quietly, with none of a care.

So let's raise our drinks, with umbrellas so bright,
Here's to the mishaps, the sun, and the fight!
With laughter and splashes, let's not take it so serious,
For moments like this can be downright hilarious.

Emerald Canopies

Underneath the green, the leaves start to sway,
A squirrel drops an acorn, what a clumsy display!
The sun peeks cheekily, between branches so thin,
As critters all scurry, like they're late for a win.

The breeze tickles noses, brings giggles and sneezes,
While nature just chuckles, the trees share their eases.
Blades of grass whisper, secrets so wild,
While bugs play charades, mischief's their style!

A picnic's laid out but ants form a line,
"Your sandwich looks tasty, we're all here to dine!"
With crumbs and confusion, the laughter does soar,
As everyone panics and makes a quick score.

In this garden of whimsy, where oddities grow,
A dancing grasshopper steals the whole show!
So raise your glass high, to the joyous and sweet,
For life under canopies can't be beat!

Sunlit Veils of Air

Clouds are like marshmallows, fluffy and bright,
While kids chase their dreams, taking flight with delight.
A squirrel in sunglasses, looking so cool,
While frogs form a band, it's quite the odd school.

A kite takes a tumble, it doesn't quite care,
It spins through the sky, like an acrobat bare.
"Catch me if you can!" it seems to declare,
While a toddler just giggles, blissfully unaware.

The sun flirts with shadows, a playful charade,
While grasshoppers chorus, they're ready to parade.
With laughs filling up, the air's pure delight,
As parents roll on, not quite ready to fight.

So here's to the fun under sunlit displays,
With peculiar antics that brighten our days!
Let's cherish this circus, the joy and the flair,
For life feels like magic up here in thin air.

Calm Currents of the Shore

The waves roll in gently, a comedic routine,
While seagulls have debates, quite raucous, I mean.
Shells are the tickets to the ocean's grand show,
As children pretend they are mermaids aglow.

Old lovers stroll hand in hand, what a sight,
While a crab pinches toes, and they leap in fright.
Flip-flops go missing, it's a wild chase at play,
As laughter erupts from the land and the bay.

Sun hats fly off, caught by the cheeky winds,
While everyone giggles at their silly spins.
The surfboards are waiting, with tales to impart,
Of waves caught in triumph, or splashes of art.

So raise up your glass, to the quirks galore,
For life at the shore is never a bore!
With laughter as bright as the sun's golden hue,
Every moment is perfect, just waiting for you.

Sunlit Moments in the Grove

Under the trees, a squirrel spun,
His acorn stash got up and run.
Lizards laugh, they dance and dart,
While I just sit, a lazy part.

Coconuts drop, a thud and roll,
A playful game, we lose control.
Dancing shadows twist and sway,
As sunlight winks, it's here to play.

Birds mock the breeze with silly tunes,
As if they think they're late for June.
Their feathers ruffle, they prance about,
Who knew a critter could scream and shout?

With every chuckle, the day goes bright,
In this bright grove, nothing feels right.
But laughter echoes, we take a chance,
With silly moments, we join the dance.

Embracing the Ocean's Breath

Waves whisper secrets, sandy surprise,
Seagulls dive in, oh, what a rise!
Surfboards tip over, folks take a fall,
Splashing the beach with giggles and all.

Flip-flops fly as kids chase the tide,
While sun-kissed mermaids try to hide.
Suntan lotion, a slippery mess,
A slippery slip, oh, such finesse!

Parents sunbathe, turning like pies,
While kids outsmart, and devise the cries.
In the sandcastles, history's made,
Until one wave's all it takes to fade.

And when the day dims, laughter remains,
With echoes of joy rolling like trains.
Oh, the ocean laughs, with a bubbly cheer,
For every splash says, "Come back next year!

Mirage of Green Against Blue

In the jungle green, a monkey swung,
He spotted a snack, and loudly sung.
His friend in a hat tried to catch the treat,
But ended up tangled in vines, what a feat!

The butterflies painted, a vibrant show,
While ants in a line march to and fro.
Tickled by petals, they dance all around,
As laughter ignites from the silliness found.

A parrot squawks, "This isn't my scene!"
While crickets hum tunes, it's rather serene.
The river flows by with a gurgling song,
But the bamboo's insistence keeps all feeling strong.

With every giggle, a story is spun,
Of tropical follies, just waiting for fun.
In mirrors of green against skies so bright,
The laughter continues, a joyful delight.

Secrets of the Tropical Air

In the stillness, a breeze comes to tease,
Leaves shaking, singing, doing their freeze.
Raccoons in masks lurk, keep to their plans,
Giggling softly, like mischievous fans.

As colors burst forth, the flowers conspire,
With bees buzzing in, it's a floral quire.
They dip and dive, trying each bloom,
And I just sit, napping on a broom.

Whispers of mischief spin 'round the trees,
While the wind carries laughter like happy bees.
A hammock swings high, and cats start to yawn,
As all through the air, silly secrets are drawn.

So here we'll stay where the fun never ends,
In this tropical world, with laughs to extend.
With giggles and snickers and joy to share,
We'll unearth the secrets within the warm air.

Whispers of the Coastal Tide

The waves laugh loudly as they crash,
Seagulls steal fries in a comical flash.
Sandcastles tumble, a sandy disgrace,
While sunburned tourists hide from their base.

Crabs in tuxedos dance to the beat,
Wiggling their claws, can't help but compete.
Shells wear hats, quite the ocean's delight,
A sandy soirée, what a hilarious sight!

Flip-flops trip over uneven ground,
Adults act like kids, laughter abound.
Tides tickle toes with a playful tease,
While fish laugh quietly, swimming with ease.

In the twilight glow where the shadows all meet,
We're all just beachgoers with sandy retreat.
As the waves whisper secrets, oh so divine,
We'll chuckle at memories, forever entwined.

Dancing Leaves Under the Sun

Leaves twirl like dancers, in a grand parade,
Chasing each other in a leafy charade.
Branches gossip with a rustling cheer,
While squirrels debate which nut to endear.

Chirping birds join in the finch-filled fun,
Squawking about who'll get a tan in the sun.
A breeze lifts a hat off a man's balding head,
He laughs as it flutters, just like the spread!

Dandelions jest with their fluffy attire,
Preparing for takeoff, in comedic desire.
Flowers wink brightly, a colorful crew,
As petals giggle, does laughter ensue?

In the warm embrace of nature's delight,
Humor blooms brightly, oh what a sight!
We share in the whimsy, a light-hearted mood,
As life dances on, in laughter renewed.

Serenity in the Shade

Under the trees where the coolness resides,
Bees tell the gossip on gentle slide rides.
A picnic's laid out, sandwiches in tow,
But ants throw a party, as munchies they stow.

The lemonade's cold, in a pitcher like gold,
While squirrels trade tales, ever so bold.
A feathered friend steals a bite of our cake,
What a raucous gathering, for goodness' sake!

A funny dog darts, too eager to roam,
Chasing after shadows with all of its foam.
Laughter erupts as a cat takes a leap,
Into the bushes, for a moment quite cheap.

In moments like these, we chuckle and play,
Finding pure joy in the shade's gentle sway.
A laughter-filled picnic, serene yet so loud,
In the arms of the trees, we happily crowd.

Gentle Zephyrs at Dusk

As the sun dips low, the colors ignite,
The sky's like a canvas, what a sight!
A playful breeze wiggles through the trees,
Tickling the branches, bending with ease.

Crickets start chirping their evening tunes,
While fireflies twinkle like tiny balloons.
A raccoon in spectacles offers a show,
With antics so silly, we can't help but go!

Shadows stretch long as the day takes a bow,
The world gets a giggle, under soft glow.
Each rustle amongst leaves, a joke that's in place,
The garden's a theater, laughter we chase.

In the fading light where the funny things dwell,
Nature invites us for one last farewell.
With each whispered chuckle, we bask in delight,
As the day takes its leave, bringing laughter to night.

Rustic Notes of Calm

In a hammock, I swing and sway,
Beneath the leaves, I snooze away.
The wind whispers secrets, oh so sly,
While squirrels plot their acorn heist nearby.

A flower sneezes, pollen takes flight,
I laugh aloud, what a funny sight!
The grass tickles toes, a playful tease,
As I bask in warmth, with utmost ease.

Oh, the joys of a lazy noon,
Where time forgets to play its tune.
The sun's a joker, with radiant beams,
And I'm just drifting, lost in dreams.

A dance of shadows, a chirpy cheer,
Nature's concert, oh so near!
With every giggle, every little hum,
Life's a chuckle, and then some!

Heartbeats of Summer Air

A cheeky breeze gives me a nudge,
I swear it's grinning, won't budge!
The kites are soaring, ragged and wild,
Like toddlers playing, so un-refiled.

The sun's a prankster, burns my nose,
While ants march proud in single rows.
They march for snacks, a feast so grand,
While I just lounge with snacks at hand.

Oh, the joy of a picnic spread,
Until a turkey sandwich's upside down, dead.
A little breeze plays footsie with the ants,
As I can't help but risk my chance.

Laughter bubbles through the golden grass,
As I watch the time creep and pass.
In this daydream, I feel alive,
Summer's a joke, we all survive!

Illusive Hues of the Horizon

Orange skies hold secrets untold,
While I pretend to be brave and bold.
The sunset smiles, what a prankster's art,
As I trip on my flip-flop, oh, what a start!

A seagull swoops, steals my fries,
Cackles loudly, oh what a surprise!
I throw my hands up, can't help but laugh,
Some days to eat are quite the gaffe.

The clouds wear hats, I swear it's true,
A cotton candy party, right for you.
I wave at the sun, my cheeky friend,
Can't wait to see what tricks he'll send.

Nature teases, with hues so bright,
While I dance like no one's in sight.
These moments capture life that gleams,
In silly colors, we find our dreams!

A Symphony of Sunlit Greens

The leaves rustle like they know a joke,
While I attempt to mimic a yoke.
I trip over roots—oh, woe is me,
This forest stage is comedy spree.

One bug wore glasses, such a sight!
Reading leaves by daylight, oh what a plight!
While I hum tunes, off-key at best,
Nature's rhythm puts me to the test.

Dandelions dance, to their own little show,
With wind's gentle push, they twirl and flow.
I join the fun, with a leaps and bounds,
Trying to catch fairies, all around.

As the sun dips low, laughter echoes wide,
In this silly garden, I'll always abide.
For life's a melody, funny and bright,
In nature's embrace, all feels right!

The Lullaby of Leaves

Whispering tales of green and sway,
A dance from branches, come what may.
The squirrels giggle, their acorn stash,
Dropping jewels with a playful crash.

Rustling softly, the trees have fun,
Telling secrets, 'til day is done.
While shadows join in with a grin,
As leafy layers let the laughter in.

Twinkle toes of the windy kind,
In the chaos, a whimsy unwind.
Nature's choir in a comical tone,
Creating jokes in a leafy zone.

So lounge awhile as the giggles unfold,
Where stories of greens and golds are told.
With every shuffle, laughter's near,
In the calm where the heart has cheer.

Breezy Embrace of Paradise

In a realm where the kookaburras giggle,
And monkeys swing with a playful wiggle.
A wind that tickles the sun-kissed cheeks,
As roosters crow, and the party peaks.

The palm fronds sway, doing a silly dance,
In this wild backyard, take a chance.
While sunbeams tickle a cheeky crab,
Everyone's sure it's no quiet blab.

A grasshopper leaps with astounding flair,
Wearing shades and a tropical glare.
While flowers bust out their worst dad jokes,
Inviting all the jubilant folks.

So grab your drink; here fun is rife,
As we party with the critters of life.
Underneath this joking sky,
All stress just skips and says goodbye.

Shadows from the Canopy

Sunlight spills through a leafy veil,
Creating characters as stories unveil.
A shadow stretches, then suddenly slips,
Causing giggles and whimsical quips.

Lizards prance in dapper suits,
As if preparing for grand parades and hoots.
While the branches wave hello and goodbye,
Sprinkling starlight from the sky.

The rustle knows all the best punchlines,
As critters swap their funny designs.
In shadows where laughter takes its flight,
Daylight wanes into the night.

Chasing shapes that dance on the ground,
With whispers of fun that echo around.
This canopy world so lively and bright,
Where humor finds its way to delight.

Mellow Zephyrs at Twilight

Evening falls with a giggling breeze,
Whirling around the palm tree leaves.
Napping crickets hum a sleepy tune,
Dreaming away 'neath the glowing moon.

A playful gust steals my cap away,
As I chase it, the stars start to play.
Fireflies flash like tiny spotlights,
In this wacky show of drowsy nights.

With whispers of joy and cozy dreams,
Nature's comedy bursts at the seams.
Joining the laughter, the owls hoot wise,
As nightfall decorates the skies.

So kick back now and embrace the chill,
While fun drifts in with a spirited thrill.
In the twilight's arms, we find our glee,
Where the evening sings, "Come laugh with me!"

Flights of Verdant Whispers

In a jungle of giggles, leaves sway,
The monkeys dance, come join the play.
A parrot squawks, trying to rhyme,
But sounds more like a clown each time.

Laughter echoes from trunk to trunk,
As turtles strut in their funky funk.
A chameleon slips, in colors he'll flash,
But trips on his tail—it's a colorful crash.

Sunshine tickles, the air's light and free,
While toucans argue, a comedy spree.
They crack silly jokes, in beaks and in flight,
Both confused by the clouds that look just like bites.

So if you hear laughter amidst the green,
It's nature's own show, a wild routine.
So grab your hats, and join the delight,
In this jungle, where humor takes flight.

In the Embrace of the Dawn

At dawn's first wink, the roosters yawn,
A cat's in a stretch, and so is a fawn.
The bees start buzzing, a morning parade,
While crickets complain they didn't get paid.

A rabbit hops in, with quite the flair,
But trips on a leaf—oh, what a scare!
The sun peeks through, with a golden smile,
Making the critters dance for a while.

Birds squawk out songs, off-key and loud,
Trying to impress a gathering crowd.
A squirrel juggles acorns, brave little champ,
But drops them all—splat! onto the lamp.

Laughter erupts as day catches fire,
While all of nature's a little bit higher.
These antics continue till night comes along,
Where shadows take part in the day's silly song.

The Nature of Serendipity

In a grove where surprises like to hide,
A flamingo prances with ridiculous pride.
He trips on a branch, tries to do a twirl,
And lands in a pond—oh, what a swirl!

A hedgehog plays poker, with no eyes to peek,
The stakes get high! It's hilarious week.
The rabbits are betting on who will win,
While a tortoise shuffles, his odds are quite thin.

Unexpected friends make laughter their game,
The sloth declares, "I'll take all the fame!"
But hanging upside down gets him quite mixed,
So a riot of giggles is how he's fixed.

At twilight's close, the fun never quits,
As fireflies switch on their glowing bits.
This circle of joy, where chance rules the day,
Is a testament to laughter in nature's own way.

Remnants of a Gentle Caress

A wisp of humor floats through the air,
As crabs do the cha-cha, without a care.
The seaweed's laughing, all tangled in knots,
And a fish wears a hat—it's the funniest plot.

The sun flips pancakes on waves that play cool,
While dolphins steal surfboards, a comical duel.
A seal cracks jokes that make sea turtles roll,
Splashes of laughter fill the entire shoal.

A pelican winks with a fish in his beak,
He munches and talks—quite the sight to seek.
While octopuses juggle, their skill on display,
As the tide changes rhythm, it's a wild ballet.

With a wink from the stars, the night follows suit,
As laughter from beaches gets wrapped in a flute.
Here joy takes a ride on the wind's sweet refrain,
A merry-go-round of chuckles, that's just how we reign.

Echoes of Nature's Serenade

When the wind starts to tattle,
Leaves begin a giggle,
Caught in whispers of sunlight,
Dancing like a wiggle.

A squirrel prances around,
In search of a lost nut,
But his jump makes him tumble,
Oh how he's in a rut!

Birds chirp jokes from the trees,
With punchlines that don't land,
Each note is quite a chuckle,
As laughter fills the land.

Nature's jokes are the best,
I chuckle at their rhymes,
Each tickle that I feel,
Is laughter that times climbs.

Tranquil Moments Beneath the Canopy

Underneath the leafy crowd,
A picnic's set with flair,
Ants are stealing the cupcake,
How rude, I do declare!

The sun peeks with a grin,
Mischief in its bright rays,
It tickles all the shadows,
In the silliest of ways.

A raccoon in the background,
Wearing shades that are too wide,
Looks like a rock star to me,
Oh, he has not much pride!

With laughter in the trees,
And snacks that disappear,
Nature's full of funny sights,
As the day shines sincere.

Whispers of the Ocean

Waves are rolling in with jokes,
Crashing on the sandy shore,
A crab joins the pun parade,
Shuffling like it's folklore.

Seagulls squawk their best punchlines,
While fishing for some bites,
They've forgotten how to fish,
In their comedy flights.

The water tickles my toes,
A splash then a giggle's born,
As the sun dips down to laugh,
It knows no night is worn.

With bubbles rising high,
Nature's humor will take flight,
Each wave a witticism,
Underneath the starlit light.

Dancing Fronds at Dusk

At twilight, fronds shake their hips,
In a dance of pure delight,
They make the finest of twirls,
Underneath the fading light.

Lizards throw a little shimmy,
With moves that might impress,
They stop to pose and laugh a bit,
In nature's fancy dress.

The moon shows off its silver glow,
Casting humor on the scene,
A palm's twist here, a kick there,
It's a dance that's quite obscene!

When dusk drops its curtain low,
And laughter fills the air,
I join with nature's folly,
In this joyful evening fare.

Nature's Emblem of Serenity

In the shade, I spied a bug,
Doing a jig, oh what a shrug!
With a twist and a flop so grand,
He could win the dance-off, oh so planned.

A squirrel chuckles, his acorn stashed,
In a secret vault, he's quickly dashed.
With a leap and a bounce, he finds delight,
Who knew nuts were such a tasty bite?

A butterfly whirls in polka dots bright,
Whispering secrets, taking flight.
While grasshoppers chirp like they know the tune,
Wiggling their legs in a funky swoon.

Looming figures, trees twisted and spry,
Trying hard to wave, oh my!
With limbs like dancers, they sway side to side,
Shaking those leaves with silly pride.

Tantalizing Tresses of Nature

The ferns are flirting, oh how they tease,
Swaying in rhythm, with the slightest breeze.
An old crow caws, sporting a hat,
Quaint fashion tips? Why, look at that!

A skunk strolls by, with a strut so grand,
Beneath the sun, like he owns this land.
All the critters, they gather round,
To hear him tell tales, the best in town.

As rivers giggle over stones so round,
They tickle the feet of all that's found.
Waves of laughter, from turtles who float,
Belly laughs echo from that old goat.

With flowers nudging their heads to play,
In a colorful dance, they brighten the day.
"Freshly picked!" one of them boasts with flair,
Hoping a bee swings by to share!

The Tender Kiss of Morn

Morning yawns with sleepy beams,
As dew drops dangle like tiny dreams.
A rooster crows, sees the sun's bright face,
Then strikes a pose, a true feathered ace.

The breeze whispers jokes through soft green grass,
While ants debate on the speed of their class.
A frog leaps up, wearing a crown made of flies,
Who knew breakfast could be such a surprise?

Clouds gather round, playing hide-and-seek,
With shadows that giggle and elfin peek.
"Hey look at me!" yells the prancing deer,
Nothin' like morning to spread some cheer!

A meadow that dances, sways and spins,
With flowers joining in, oh what begins!
A daisy pulls faces, trying to impress,
While the wind laughs outright, "You're such a mess!"

Cascade of Light through Leaves

Sunlight tumbles in a cheeky race,
Through branches that smile, no frowning face.
Tickling the turtles, as they bask in grace,
Each ray a magician, brightening the space.

A light dusting of chips from the pines,
Makes the squirrels think they're drawing designs.
With crafty paws, they sketch sights unmatched,
A masterpiece made, and they're quite attached.

A curtain of green, where shadows play,
Crickets serenade towards the end of day.
As butterflies flutter, they cancel all maps,
Getting lost in the dance, oh what mishaps!

A golden hour, so vibrant and bold,
Nature's jester playing tricks old.
With a giggle and wink from every vine,
They plot to make dull days all divine!

Celestial Drift Amongst Greenery

The sunbeams dance, they flirt and play,
While leaves swing low in a funny way.
If trees could giggle, they'd surely laugh,
As squirrels perform their acrobatic half.

A butterfly sneezes, then takes a spin,
Pollinating flowers with a cheeky grin.
The shadows gossip, shading the ants,
Whispering secrets of their wild prance.

A bird with style sings off-key,
Dropping beats like it's trying to flee.
With twirls and swirls, the grass sings loud,
Leaving the daisies quite unbowed.

Sunshine tickles, it plays all day,
While laughter erupts in a light-hearted way.
In this verdant haven, joy is found,
As nature jests, and laughter abounds.

Vistas of Vivid Dreams

Clouds are jesters in this bright show,
As raindrops tumble, putting on a glow.
With earthy scents that dance in the air,
The sun winks, a cheeky little dare.

Rainbow slides for the birds to glide,
They dive and dip, without a guide.
A squirrel in shades, stylishly spry,
Practices moves as though in the sky.

Each flower's a smile, blooming with glee,
While they plot to throw a grand jamboree.
The breeze tells jokes to the tall, wise trees,
Who chuckle and swish, flowing like these.

In this playful stretch of endless green,
Nature shares humor rarely seen.
With every twist and turn that we seek,
A world so funny, it makes us squeak!

Aloft Between the Trees

Swinging vines with a witty twist,
Invite the squirrels to join the list.
They chatter about the acorn's fate,
While leaves above hold a secret state.

A frog with dreams of flying high,
Practices jumps that seem to defy.
Old man oak chuckles a hearty laugh,
As branches sway, composing a gaff.

Crickets chirp in a comedic tune,
Singing loud to the curious moon.
With each rustle, nature's cheeky wit,
Makes even the trees want to join in a skit.

As twilight drops its shimm'ring veil,
Laughter echoes on the evening trail.
For here, among the leaves and the pines,
The humor of life is where joy aligns.

The Language of Gentle Currents

Waves flap their arms, waving hello,
To fishes who dance with quite the show.
A turtle tumbles, a splashy plight,
As ripples giggle in pure delight.

The sun nods off for a short nap,
While shadows conspire to form a map.
Whispers of jokes float on the breeze,
Where laughter morphs into soft pleas.

Even the rocks have punchlines to share,
Cracking wise in a placid flare.
A crab with a hat struts by with flair,
Snapping a selfie without a care.

The currents laugh, in a playful swirl,
Tickling the shores in a joyful whirl.
In this silly world, where echoes reside,
Nature crackles with humor, full of pride.

Rhapsody of Waves and Green

Under the sun, with hats too wide,
Waves tickle feet, we shuffle aside.
Laughter erupts, a splash and a scream,
While seaweed dances, like it's in a dream.

Seagulls squawk with a gossiping glee,
Trying to steal chips, oh, how cheeky!
Flip-flops gone rogue, they soar through the sky,
As we chase after them, oh my, oh my!

Sunscreen's on, but wait, what a mess!
I now resemble a lumpy white dress.
With arms like butter and legs like jam,
The crabs point and laugh, 'Is that really Graham?'

Jokes in the air, like kites in a swirl,
Tangled together, oh what a twirl.
As we picnic and giggle with crumbs in our hair,
Life's a funny dance, without a care.

Secrets in the Moving Air

Whispers of laughter float on a breeze,
Socks on the line, waving with ease.
Windsock a-flying, it's quite a sight,
Who knew that laundry could take flight?

Kites and confetti, all tangled and stuck,
A chase after snacks—the true form of luck.
Garden gnomes chuckle at the antics unwind,
As squirrels hold meetings—are they plotting or kind?

Ants in formation, quite the parade,
Stealing our food, oh how they invade!
One brave little bug takes a leap with flair,
Slips on a chip, and lands in mid-air!

But through it all, we giggle and cheer,
For nature's a circus, come take a peer.
As we bask in the chaos, the fun, and the play,
Life's little secrets, waiting each day.

Sun-Kissed Silhouettes

Shadows are wobbling, making us grin,
A crab clapped its claws, 'Let's all join in!'
With sandals akimbo and sunburned noses,
We strut like the stars, in wild poses.

Tanned from adventures, full of good cheer,
Sunblock's our armor, and laughter's our gear.
Belly flops await, with splashes and yells,
While floaties race like they're under some spells.

Sipping refreshments, so fruity, so bright,
The straws tango wildly, what a silly sight!
Who dropped the pickle in the lemonade glass?
Oh wait, that's just Uncle with no class!

With dusk drawing nigh, we gather and shake,
The shadows now wiggle, as the fireflies wake.
The moon gives a wink, with a chuckle so sweet,
As we all spin around, dancing on our feet.

Lattice of Light and Shade

Dappled light flickers, beneath branches wide,
Chasing around, no reason to hide.
A picnic blanket forms a portly ship,
As ants launch an ambush—oh my, a trip!

Shade gives us refuge, from sun's hot embrace,
Yet it also offers a mysterious place.
A squirrel dives in, fluffs up and declares,
'This feast is for critters, better beware!'

We launch grapes into the air with delight,
Who knew they could bounce like a soft out of sight?
Laughter erupts as they roll away fast,
While a raccoon scoffs and makes a bold cast.

So gather your friends, in laughter and play,
Under the lattice, we twist and we sway.
In the warmth of the day, with revels untamed,
Life's a jolly party, we're all entertained.

Dappled Light Through Canopies

In a dance of light they sway,
The green hats greet the day.
Squirrels join the jolly chase,
While I trip on roots with grace.

Sunbeams wiggle through the leaves,
Casting shadows where one grieves.
A squirrel's leap, a casual snack,
Leaves me wondering, what's the knack?

Branches shake with giggles sweet,
As they whisper 'take a seat!'
But watch your back, oh clumsy friend,
A rogue nut might just descend!

When dusk descends with twinkling light,
The leaves all whisper, "What a sight!"
I wave goodbye with a loud cheer,
"See you all again, my dear!"

Carefree Days of Gentle Currents

Under smiles of shining sun,
We laugh until the day is done.
With hats that fly and shoes that splash,
Tickling toes while time does dash.

A stroll beside the stream so bright,
Where rambunctious fish take flight.
We toss our snacks and giggle loud,
While ducklings form their little crowd.

Bologna sandwiches take the throne,
A lunch so silly, all alone!
Yet ants march in, uninvited too,
Comedians in black, what a crew!

As twilight paints the world so grand,
We toast to days that were well planned.
With veggie sticks and laughter's cheer,
We'll do it all again next year!

Serenity's Embrace

In a corner of nature's glee,
A hammock hangs just for me.
But as I swing, I toss and turn,
A moth's wild dance makes me spurn.

The slumber's sweet, or so it seems,
Till twigs crack, and I wake from dreams.
With blanket snug around my chin,
I smile as ants parade on in.

"Hey, little friends, what's the rush?"
They line up fast in quite a hush.
A picnic crasher? Don't you dare!
Or I will launch a fluff-filled air!

Now evening's glow begins to fade,
I laugh and reminisce my raid.
With dreams of snacks, I sway with glee,
What fun this life, so wild and free!

The Language of Soft Winds

Whispers float on air so light,
Carrying secrets, oh what a sight!
Tickles of laughter in every tree,
As squirrels debate their comedy.

A tall palm calls, "Dance with me!"
But I trip over roots, you see.
The leaves all chuckle in their way,
As I march on, in pure dismay.

Sunset colors swirl and sway,
While critters perform a cabaret.
I clap too loud, get shushed by night,
But I can't help; it feels so right!

So here's to joy in every gust,
To playful flirts and joyous thrust.
With laughter high and spirits free,
The world's a stage for you and me!

Soft Whispers from the Island Heart

A puff of wind gives a cheeky grin,
Causing hats to fly and dance in spin.
The sun laughs out in a golden glare,
While seagulls squawk as if they care.

A coconut drops like a clumsy mime,
And folks all chuckle at the funny rhyme.
Palm trees sway with a jolly jig,
While tourists stumble, looking quite big!

Come join the game of tree trunk tag,
Where trunks are proud and roots just brag.
The island's charm is a giddy tune,
Playing soft songs that make you swoon.

Under this sky, with laughter's spark,
Life is a stroll in the park's remark.
The heart of the island beats with a laugh,
In its silly whirl, we find our path.

Elysian Rustle in the Cove

In a hidden nook where giggles play,
A rustle shares secrets in a quirky way.
Leaves wiggle, chuckling at the tide,
While crabs make faces, scuttling wide.

Above, the clouds throw a misty pink,
As dolphins leap, with a wink and blink.
A splash is heard like a jest unplanned,
While sunbathers giggle, sunbaked and tanned.

Tidal waves tease with a ticklish push,
That sends one diving in an awkward rush.
The water's alive with a frothy cheer,
As laughter rings out, far and near.

With sandy toes and a playful air,
Every heart's light, floating without care.
The cove is a haven where joy is rife,
In this enchanted place, we dance with life.

Dreaming Under the Arching Canopy

Beneath the green where shadows play,
The trees tell tales in a breezy sway.
A lizard sunbathes with a wink so sly,
While ants march on like they're aiming high.

The whispers of the leaves, a tone of glee,
As they gossip about the buzzing bee.
"Was that a sneeze?" the flowers all muse,
Flapping their petals with colorful views.

A squirrel, bold, in acrobatic leaps,
While chasing the wind and dodging the creeps.
Each rustle and shuffle brings guffaws around,
In this canopy's grip, no worries are found.

With laughter aloft on branches so fair,
This shady haven casts away despair.
Among the laughers, dreams grow bright,
In nature's embrace, all feels just right.

The Solace of Sway

In the gentle sway of a happy dance,
The world spins 'round in a joyful romance.
Old trees chuckle at the antics of the breeze,
While monkeys grin, swinging with ease.

The sunbeams play tag, flickering bright,
As they tease the flowers, their petals in flight.
A frisbee sails with a triumphant shout,
While it lands in the palms—what's that about?

With smiles like sunshine, the children dart,
Together they craft this whimsical art.
Every gust brings a mischievous call,
As laughter erupts through the palm-spattered hall.

So raise a glass to the winds that play,
To the tales that twist in a merry ballet.
In the solace of sway, all worries cease,
And the heart of the island finds its peace.

Serene Winds Beneath the Sun

A gust came by, it blew my hat,
It danced away, oh where's it at?
The seagulls laughed, they found it too,
While I just stood there, feeling blue.

My shirt flew up, it joined the fun,
Twisting like a fish just caught on a run.
Oh, the shade beneath the tree looked sweet,
But my snack became a treat for feet!

A cocktail spilled, and what a mess,
It splashed on me with such finesse.
The drink I bought was nearly gone,
Just like my chance at a calm dawn!

I hugged a palm, gave it a grin,
It swayed back slowly, acting like kin.
Next time I'll wear a weighted cap,
So nothing leaves me—just take a nap!

Tropical Reverie

A playful breeze tickled my nose,
I sneezed so loud, it scared the crows.
They chirped in shock, then took to the skies,
Leaving me laughing, oh what a surprise!

The sun shone bright with gleeful flair,
While I spilled sunscreen all through my hair.
Bottles flew like rockets so bold,
My hair turned sticky, a sight to behold!

With every step, the sand stuck tight,
My flip-flops squeaked, what a funny sight.
An iguana joined with flair of style,
He winked at me with a humorous smile!

A coconut dropped, right on my shoe,
It rolled away as if it knew!
I laughed so hard, I clutched my chest,
This island life is truly the best!

Echoes of the Coastline

The waves whispered jokes to rocks on the shore,
They giggled and chuckled, always wanting more.
A crab waved at me, thought he was slick,
But snapped his own claw, oh that's quite a trick!

I built a sandcastle, tall and grand,
But a wave came crashing, oh what was planned?
My turrets fell with a funny splat,
I shrugged and thought, "Well, how about that?"

In the distance, a dolphin leaped high,
Did a flip and a dip, caught the sun in the sky.
I clapped and cheered, "What a great show!"
But then slipped on wet sand, down I did go!

With laughter echoing up and down the coast,
I made new friends—oh, that's what I boast!
We danced on the foamy waves at dusk,
Silly smiles shared, oh, that's a must!

Swaying Dreams of Summer

The swaying trinkets of the palm trees,
Gave me a tickle, like funnypeas.
They laughed as I tried to catch a breeze,
But only found my sunglasses with ease!

A wind-up toy, my kite took flight,
It zoomed away, oh what a sight!
Chasing my dreams, or so I thought,
But the tree caught it, such a crafty plot!

I set out a picnic, with goodies galore,
But ants threw a party, oh what a chore!
They marched right in, no invitation sent,
With tiny plates and a feast they spent!

With every giggle, the day slipped away,
As I danced in shadows of palm fronds swayed.
A summer so funny, I'll laugh till I drop,
In memories of joy, the silliness won't stop!

The Elegance of Soft Air

A waft of fluff, a tickle too,
Dancing hats chased by a shoe.
Laughter floats on feathery tones,
While sunburned folks protect their bones.

Umbrellas flip, they take to flight,
As seagulls giggle with delight.
A soft nudge to the gentle sway,
Oops! There goes my soda tray!

Flip-flops squeak with every step,
The grand parade of warm indebt.
With every gust, a cheeky grin,
Who doesn't love a cheeky spin?

So when the warmth begins to play,
Embrace the quirks of sunny day.
And as you tread on sandy ground,
Remember laughter knows no bound.

Tropical Serenade

A gentle hum like buzzing bees,
As palm leaves wave, they bend their knees.
Sunglasses perched, they start to dance,
While coconuts plot their romance.

At beachside bars, the drinks are tall,
But watch that wave! It may just stall.
A splash, a laugh, a tales to tell,
When sea foam acts like a jester's spell.

Fruits stacked high in a wobbly mound,
Each slice a joke that's quite profound.
With every bite, a nugget wise,
A fruity grin beneath the skies.

But as the dusk brings on a chill,
A sunset hues, a laughter's thrill.
So raise a toast, my friends, and cheer,
For sunny days will reappear!

Sailors' Breath of Freedom

A salty breeze with a cheeky wink,
A sailor's hat floats past the sink.
Waves that laugh as boats go by,
With seagulls swooping low and high.

The captain's pipe – a song off-key,
Dancing nets, they jig with glee.
A splash of spray, a friendly sting,
Oops! There goes the meat for spring!

Fish that leap to steal the show,
While cowboys of the sea say 'Whoa!'
Each buoy bobs as if it knows,
That sea legs bend in endless 'whoas'.

So raise the sail, let laughter sail,
Adventure's breeze is never stale.
A pirate's life, they claim with pride,
Just don't forget – there's a joyride!

Whispering Palettes of Nature

Colors swirl amidst the scene,
Nature paints with a cheeky sheen.
Each leaf a brush, each petal's wink,
Serenading what we think.

Whispers float from trees so tall,
As critters plot a sneaky brawl.
Oh, what's that? A dance-off planned,
As flowers clap – oh, isn't it grand?

The rustle of joy, leaves spin around,
While daisies laugh on grassy ground.
With every gust, a funny play,
Nature's fun is here to stay.

So step into this vivid land,
Where whimsy grows as nature's hand.
In every shade, a chuckle lies,
A masterpiece of bright blue skies.

Revered Harmony of the Tropics

The leaves are whispering in a cheeky tone,
As critters in the shade are rolling on their own.
A lizard dons a hat, oh what a sight,
While squirrels compete in a nutty flight.

Bananas giggle high, just out of reach,
Coconuts in the corner, each a beach.
A parrot cracks a joke, loud as can be,
While turtles tune in, enjoying the spree.

Rusty pipes and planks make music so odd,
As goats on the hills perform a dance prod.
The sun throws confetti on everything fine,
Each creature chuckling, they all sip divine.

With jigs and jives, the dance floor is set,
No one can sit still, oh no, not just yet!
A standstill is banned, while the sun stays bright,
Join the fun in this tropical delight!

Surreal Dancing Shadows

Underneath the neon glow of night,
The shadows strut their stuff, what a sight!
A crab with shades is leading the pack,
While a glowworm's disco gives them the knack.

Palm fronds twist and shout in twilight's glow,
Spinning like they've got a show to throw.
The moon's got rhythm, a DJ so sly,
Bats do the cha-cha in the starlit sky.

A frog in a tux strikes a pose so grand,
While snails do the slide, a slow-motion band.
The breeze plays a tune that can't be beat,
And even the crickets join in with their beat.

As dawn peeks in, with a smile so wide,
The shadows retreat, but they won't hide.
For as night falls again, they'll take to the floor,
With moves that will leave you begging for more!

Secrets Beneath the Canopy

In the quiet hush, the vines start to chat,
About a missing shoe, or maybe a cat.
A sloth in a hammock is telling a tale,
Bout a lost rubber duck sailing on a trail.

The roots twitch and tangle, like playful sprites,
While beetles gossip about the wild nights.
A shy snake with a bowtie waits with flair,
For a tango partner—if anyone dare!

Fireflies giggle, they're the light brigade,
As shadows tiptoe in this leafy parade.
Each corner hides wonders, so much to find,
The laughter of nature is truly aligned.

So come and explore, let your heart sing,
For the secrets of green are a funny thing.
In the dance of the leaves, joy weaves a net,
A world full of chuckles, you'll never forget!

Golden Hour in Paradise

When the sun greets the sky, the laughter begins,
As seagulls narrate tales of their wins.
A fish with sunglasses is catching a wave,
While crabs in a conga line misbehave.

The sand gets tickled by tiny quick toes,
As flip-flops fly high, in comical throws.
Beach balls bounce wild, with shouts of delight,
In this golden hour, every moment is bright.

A monkey in shorts swings with flair,
Daring friends to join in this lively affair.
With laughter contagious beneath the warm sun,
Even coconuts join in, basking in fun!

Join the party where joy knows no bounds,
In every grin, and the comedic sounds.
For in this paradise, where the sun does glow,
Life's a funny show, just go with the flow!

Sun-Kissed Serenity

On a beach where laughter spreads,
Seagulls drop in for bread,
Sunglasses perched, looking cool,
While kids run near the pool.

The sun does a funny dance,
As flip-flops miss their chance,
A sand castle meets a wave,
Oh, how the sea can misbehave!

Boys dig trenches, find some crabs,
Sneaky shells in playful jabs,
A picnic grows legs and leaves,
With ants planning grand thieves.

Underneath the sun's big grin,
Everyone's wearing a silly spin,
So grab a snack and take a seat,
For this fun in the sun can't be beat!

Harmonies of the Sunlit Grove

In a grove where shadows play,
Squirrels have their own ballet,
A breeze tickles a big, green leaf,
As birds join in, to sing relief.

A blossom waves with flair and pride,
While bees zip by, like they're on a ride,
Laughter echoes, blending sweet,
As kids play hide-and-seek on feet.

A watermelon, round and bright,
Rolls away in sheer delight,
Chasing giggles, down the lane,
Nature's joke, a fun refrain.

So here beneath the sun's warm glow,
Life's little quirks put on a show,
With playful hearts and silly schemes,
This grove fuels our wildest dreams!

Reflections on a Gentle Tide

The waves whisper secrets, so sublime,
As crabs wear hats, oh what a crime!
A surfboard slips, the giggles flow,
While seashells blush, they steal the show.

Flip-flops squeak on sandy ground,
A floaty's lost, and we surround,
With splashes creating jokes anew,
And every wave sings just for you.

Tide pools hide tiny fishy pranks,
Curly tails and wiggly flanks,
Oh what fun to splash and glide,
With laughter riding every tide!

So here we toast to sun-kissed days,
With funny tales and Ocean's ways,
The tide reveals life's charming cheer,
In every wave, a joy sincere!

The Lullaby of Graceful Fronds

In the green where laughter spins,
Leaves sway gently, counting wins,
The sun peeks through, with a wink,
While chubby bugs give us a blink.

A lizard strikes a silly pose,
As breezy whispers tickle toes,
In dappled light, the shadows dance,
And wiggly friends all take a chance.

A picnic spreads with jelly beans,
Squirrels munch their offbeat scenes,
We giggle at the clumsy ants,
Who march in lines without any chants.

So relax amidst this leafy spree,
Where nature spins its riddle spree,
A lullaby of laughter hums,
In heart and soul, the joy just drums!

Rustling Echoes of the Shore

The coconut sings to the gulls on high,
Telling tales of the fruit that gets way too shy.
Swaying with laughter, the tall ones lean,
They dance in the wind like a playful scene.

They sway like dancers with silly poses,
Giggling at tourists who poke at roses.
"Hey, you can't pick us!" they whisper in glee,
While sunburned heads nod, sipping iced tea.

The sand plays tricks with the flip-flops on feet,
A treasure map leading to a lost little treat.
The crabs march by, all in line with chic hats,
While humans chase shadows, swatting at gnats.

So here on this shore, let laughter take wing,
With winks from the leaves, they delight in the spring.
Join in the fun, let your worries unwind,
In this land of mirth, leave the gloomy behind.

Tropic Reverie

Monkeys throw coconuts, aiming for fun,
Dodging the sun while they prank everyone.
Chasing each other with giggles galore,
It's a circus of chaos on this sandy floor.

The lizards wear sunglasses, rocking their style,
As they lounge on warm rocks with a crocodile smile.
"Is it hot out here or just us, my friend?"
They ponder the questions that never quite end.

Palm fronds do theater, swaying in play,
Telling comedic tales of a very odd day.
An octopus juggles in the nearby bay,
While dolphins perform their ballet of spray.

With rhythms of laughter, the setting sun glows,
As night brings a blanket of shimmering prose.
Join the mirthful dance under starry nets,
In this lively plot, there are no regrets.

Nature's Caress at Sunset

The sun throws a party, painting the sky,
While breezes blow kisses as fireflies fly.
The flowers are gossiping, blushing with pride,
Whispering secrets they've kept deep inside.

The frogs in tuxedos croak songs of delight,
As the moon gives a wink, peeking out at night.
"Do you hear that?" croaks a suave little chap,
"It's the rhythm of nature—now let's take a nap!"

The turtles on shells wear dazzling bright ties,
As they crawl to the beat of their own lullabies.
With smiles all around, they shuffle and glide,
"Life's a grand joke, let's take it in stride!"

With petals and laughter, this scene will remain,
As sweet moments echo like drops of warm rain.
So snuggle up close, let's lay down our fears,
In this whimsical world, we can giggle for years!

The Rhythm of Golden Leaves

The wind plays a tune on the trees overhead,
Tickling the branches and rustling their bed.
Golden leaves chuckle, all swirling and free,
"Dance with us now, come and join in our spree!"

Squirrels in top hats join in with a cheer,
Swapping their acorns for a bit of good beer.
They load up the branches, it's quite the grand feast,
With nuts flying high, the party's released.

When shadows play tag in the setting sun's hue,
The leaves drop their worries, swirling on cue.
Each turn brings a giggle, a jaunty macabre,
As they hustle and bustle on this vibrant cabaret.

So raise up your voices, let laughter transcend,
As we toast to the follies — here's to our friends!
In nature's embrace, let's dance till we drop,
In this playful ballet, the fun will not stop!

www.ingramcontent.com/pod-product-compliance
Lightning Source LLC
Chambersburg PA
CBHW072124070526
44585CB00016B/1545